THE CHEMISTRY OF EVERYDAY ELEMENTS

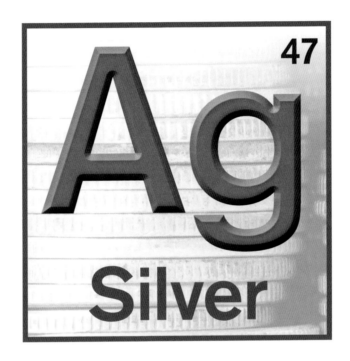

Ag 47

Silver

By Mari Rich

Mason Crest

450 Parkway Drive, Suite D
Broomall, PA 19008
www.masoncrest.com

© 2018 by Mason Crest, an imprint of National Highlights, Inc.

Printed and bound in the United States of America.

Series ISBN: 978-1-4222-3837-0
Hardback ISBN: 978-1-4222-3845-5
EBook ISBN: 978-1-4222-7950-2

33614080678930

First printing
1 3 5 7 9 8 6 4 2

Produced by Shoreline Publishing Group LLC
Santa Barbara, California
Editorial Director: James Buckley Jr.
Designer: Patty Kelley
www.shorelinepublishing.com

Library of Congress Cataloging-in-Publication Data on file with the Publisher.

Cover photographs by Dreamstime.com: Eshmadeva (left); Fireflyphoto (center); Pawel Opaska (right); Steve Heap (background).

QR Codes disclaimer:

You may gain access to certain third party content ("Third-Party Sites") by scanning and using the QR Codes that appear in this publication (the "QR Codes"). We do not operate or control in any respect any information, products, or services on such Third-Party Sites linked to by us via the QR Codes included in this publication, and we assume no responsibility for any materials you may access using the QR Codes. Your use of the QR Codes may be subject to terms, limitations, or restrictions set forth in the applicable terms of use or otherwise established by the owners of the Third-Party Sites. Our linking to such Third-Party Sites via the QR Codes does not imply an endorsement or sponsorship of such Third-Party Sites, or the information, products, or services offered on or through the Third-Party Sites, nor does it imply an endorsement or sponsorship of this publication by the owners of such Third-Party Sites.

KEY ICONS TO LOOK FOR

Words to Understand: These words with their easy-to-understand definitions will increase the reader's understanding of the text, while building vocabulary skills.

Sidebars: This boxed material within the main text allows readers to build knowledge, gain insights, explore possibilities, and broaden their perspectives by weaving together additional information to provide realistic and holistic perspectives.

Educational Videos: Readers can view videos by scanning our QR codes, providing them with additional educational content to supplement the text. Examples include news coverage, moments in history, speeches, iconic moments, and much more!

Text-Dependent Questions: These questions send the reader back to the text for more careful attention to the evidence presented here.

Research Projects: Readers are pointed toward areas of further inquiry connected to each chapter. Suggestions are provided for projects that encourage deeper research and analysis.

Series Glossary of Key Terms: This back-of-the-book glossary contains terminology used throughout this series. Words found here increase the reader's ability to read and comprehend higher-level books and articles in this field.

Introduction

When you woke up this morning and got ready to start your day, did you look in the mirror? Did you put on a favorite piece of jewelry before having some breakfast? If you were in a hurry, perhaps you just quickly shoveled in some cereal with a big spoon while checking your cell phone for text messages. You were able to do all of that because of elements.

Every single thing around you—the solids, liquids, and gases—is composed of elements of the periodic table. The periodic table is an arrangement of all the naturally occurring,

---

WORDS TO UNDERSTAND

isotope an atom of a specific element that has a different number of neutrons; it has the same atomic number but a different atomic mass

---

No picture, no people, no book, no readers—without the help of elements.

and manufactured, elements known to humans at this point in time. An element is a substance that cannot be broken down into other, separate, substances. There are 92 elements that can be found naturally on Earth and in space. The remaining 26 (and counting) have been manufactured and analyzed in a laboratory setting. These elements, alone or in combination with others, form and shape all the matter around us. From the air we breathe, to the water we drink, to the food we eat—all these things are made of elements. (As you'll soon see, your mirror, jewelry, spoon, and phone have one particular element in common!)

We can learn a lot about an element just by finding its location on the periodic table. The periodic table has undergone several updates

and reorganizations since it was first developed in 1869, until it became the modern version of the table used today. The periodic table is arranged into rows and columns by increasing atomic number. Each element has a unique atomic number. It is the number of protons in the nucleus of the atom. For example, helium has an atomic number of 2—there are two protons in the nucleus of an atom of helium. (All samples of an element have the same number of protons, but they may have a different number of neutrons in the nucleus. Atoms with

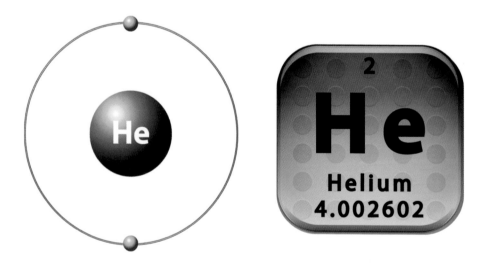

The diagram on the left shows the two protons of helium. On the right, the number at the bottom is the atomic weight of an atom of the element.

Periodic Table

The Periodic Table of the Elements is arranged in numerical order. The number of each element is determined by the number of protons in its nucleus. The horizontal rows are called periods. The number of the elements increases across a period, from left to right. The vertical columns are called groups. Groups of elements share similar characteristics. The colors, which can vary depending on the way the creators design their version of the chart, also create related collections of elements, such as noble gases, metals, or nonmetals, among others.

the same number of protons but different number of neutrons are called **isotopes**.)

Each element on the periodic table is unique, having its own chemical and physical properties. Certain chemical properties can be interpreted based on which group or row an element is placed. The periodic table also gives important information such as the number of

Silver sometimes is formed into bars, which are stamped with their purity levels.

protons and neutrons in the nucleus of one atom of an element, the number of electrons that surround the nucleus, the atomic mass, and the general size of the atom. It is also possible to predict which state of matter an element is designated by a chemical symbol—the letters that represent the element. The periodic table is a very useful tool as one begins to investigate chemistry and science in general. (For lots more on the periodic table, read *Understanding the Periodic Table*, another book in this series.)

This book is about the element silver. Silver, which has been highly prized for centuries, has 47 protons and 47 electrons. Silver is a solid under standard conditions.

How is silver a part of our lives? It's what turns a piece of glass into a mirror, to give one everyday example, and some of your jewelry might contain the soft, shiny metal. Because it was used in the past to make U.S. currency, you may even own a few old silver coins. You might not realize that silver is also a component in many electronic devices, appliances, medicines, and other products that we regularly count on. Modern life, as we know it, would be very different without silver.

Ag 47

Silver

WORDS TO UNDERSTAND

alchemist a person who practiced a science that was used in the Middle Ages that had the goal of transforming ordinary metals into gold

alloy a metal formed by combining two or more elements

archaeologist a scientist who studies human history through the artifacts left by ancient people

lode a supply of ore that is embedded between layers of rock

ore a type of rock from which a metal or mineral can be extracted

slag heap a hill made from the waste material from a mine

Discovery and History

Some elements have interesting or exciting stories connected to their discovery. For example, phosphorus, which can be found on the periodic table at number 15, was identified in 1669 by German **alchemist** Hennig Brand. He was attempting to find the philosopher's stone, a legendary object that was said to be capable of turning metals like lead and iron into gold. During one experiment, Brand boiled down 1,500 gallons of urine that he had somehow gathered from the beer drinkers in his town. The result was a waxy, light-colored substance that glowed in the dark. While he had not found the secret of making gold, Brand had discovered a new element. He named it phosphorus, which is what ancient peoples called the planet Venus. That name came from

Silver

47

Ag

The early Anatolian people who left this statue also mined silver.

the Greek words *phôs* (light) and *phoros* (bearer).

There are no colorful stories like that about silver. That's because people discovered it and began using it in prehistoric times—before events got written down.

In the Beginning

Archaeologists believe that silver was first mined more than 5,000 years ago. They have discovered **slag heaps** near ancient mines in Greece and Asia Minor. (Asia Minor was also known as Anatolia, and that area now makes up modern-day Turkey.) Experts think that silver was one of the first metals discovered and used by humans. Other early discoveries are gold, copper, lead, and iron.

Ancient Greek city-states used coins made from silver.

By 2000 BCE, it was very common for people to mine silver-bearing **ores**. The silver was extracted from the ore by heating it to a very high temperature. This process is called smelting. Smelting ore results in an impure product called an **alloy**. Alloys could be refined further through a process called cupellation. Cupellation was first developed by the ancient Chaldeans—people who lived in southeast Babylonia between the ninth and sixth centuries BCE. The melted silver was heated even further in a porous, shallow vessel known as a cupel. A strong blast of extremely hot air was blown over the cupel in a special furnace. Any impurities in the alloy were either vaporized or absorbed into the tiny pores of the cupel, leaving pure silver behind. Archae-

ologists have found many ancient objects that were made of silver refined from lead-containing ores, because silver and lead are often found together in nature.

Building Empires

Even thousands of years ago, silver was highly prized. In fact, the Greeks (and later the Romans) used wealth from silver to finance their

The United States has minted silver coins since the earliest days of the Republic.

Silver history

mighty empires, including paying for fleets of warships and building monuments.

One very well known group of mines was located near Athens, Greece. These are called the Laurium mines, and scientists have figured out that they were in operation from about 600 or 500 BCE all the way up to 100 CE. The mines were the property of the city of Athens, and they were rented out to ambitious businessmen in exchange for a portion of the silver that was obtained. The hard work of extracting the ore from underground was done by slaves. The greatest amount of silver in the Laurium mines was produced during the Classical Era (between about 480 and 323 BCE), but mining there continued on and off for centuries. The ancient Romans won control of mines in Spain during the Second Punic War (218–201 BCE), and those became major sources of silver as well. Silver from the Spanish mines was vital to trade along the Silk Road. The Silk Road was a network of trade routes, sometimes called the spice routes, stretching from China to the Mediterranean Sea.

Both the Greeks and Romans used silver to form coins. The Greek coin we know as the Athenian Tetradrachmon was the main form of

Ag
47
Silver

Silver Roman denarii (more than one denarius) came in different sizes and weights.

currency in the region during the Classical Era. The Romans used a silver coin called the denarius.

After the Moors invaded Spain in 711, knowledge of silver mining spread widely. During the Medieval period, Germany was a main source of silver, and many other mines were opened throughout Europe between 750 and 1200.

A Whole New World

Historians say that the most important date for anyone studying silver is 1492, when European explorers landed in the New World. Spanish conquerors soon found that South America had rich supplies of silver ore, and between 1500 and 1800, an estimated 85 percent of the world's silver came from mines in Bolivia, Peru, and Mexico. Today, there have been many advances in technology that make it easier than ever to mine for and refine silver. Scientists and inventors are continually finding new uses for the versatile metal. In Chapter 4, you will learn about some of those uses.

While other areas of the world—including Australia, Japan, Russia, and Canada—have been home to large silver mines, one of the most famous of recent times was discovered in 1857 in Nevada. The original discovery of silver in prehistoric times might never have been recorded, but *whole books* have been written about Nevada's massive Comstock **Lode**. Brothers named Evan and Hosea Grosh originally found the lode, but before they could officially record their claim or start mining any metals, they both died gruesome deaths. Hosea impaled his foot on a pick, and was killed by the infection that resulted. Shortly after that, Evan was caught in a snowstorm while trying to cross the Sierras. His feet froze and

Sheets of silver can be bonded to other metals to make silver plate.

Searching for gold, the Comstocks struck silver.

became infected, and he died after refusing to have them amputated.

After their deaths, Henry Comstock, a handyman who helped care for the brothers' cabin, tried unsuccessfully to find gold on their property, and he also died without becoming wealthy. (The lode is named after him anyway.) Other miners believed, like Comstock, that the lode contained gold, and they continued to mine on the property. While their dreams of gold went unfulfilled, there, in the blue clay, was enough silver to make many men rich. Prospectors from all over flocked to Nevada to get their share. A town called Virginia City sprang up on top of the Comstock Lode, with a six-story hotel, more than 100 saloons, and 20 music halls and theaters. Within a decade, the mines had produced more than $200 million worth of silver, some of which was spent financing the Civil War.

 Text-Dependent Questions

1. When was silver first mined?

2. What were the Laurium mines?

3. What country was a main source of silver during the Medieval Period?

Research Project

Between 1500 and 1800, an estimated 85 percent of the world's silver came from mines in Bolivia, Peru, and Mexico. Try to find images of silver items that were made in those countries during that period. How are they different from silver items used by the Ancient Greeks and Romans?

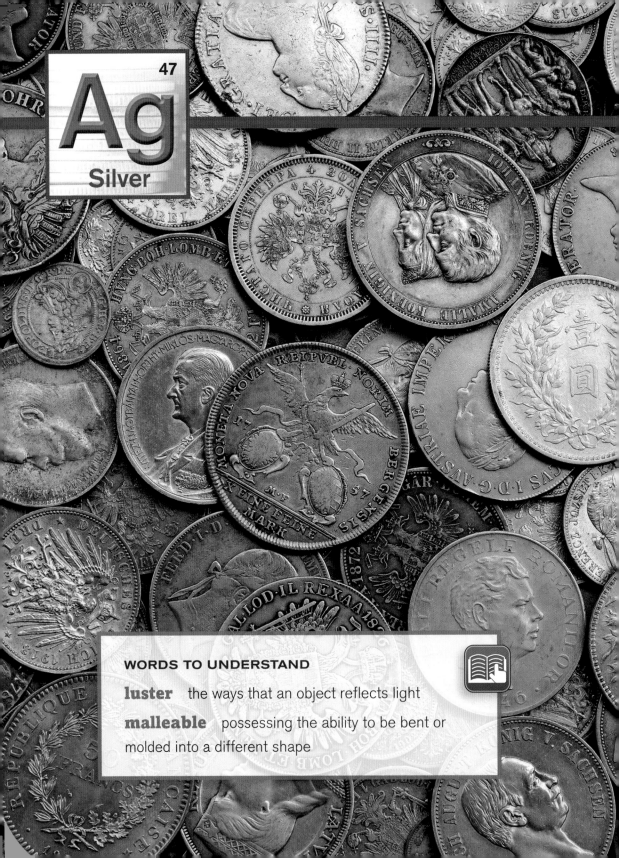

Ag
Silver
47

WORDS TO UNDERSTAND

luster   the ways that an object reflects light

malleable   possessing the ability to be bent or molded into a different shape

Chemical Properties

I f you look at the periodic table for silver, you might expect it to be represented by the letters Si. You will find, however, that Si stands for element number 14, silicon. Silver is represented by the letters Ag instead. That's really an abbreviation of the Latin word for silver, *argentum*. The Latin word was derived from a Sanskrit word, *argunas*, which means shining. Before the modern chemical symbols were created, silver was represented by a crescent-moon shape, because its **luster** reminded chemists of a glowing moon.

Like the other elements in group 11 of the periodic table, silver is a metal. The others are copper (number 29), gold (79), and roentgenium (111). Like many of the other metals in groups 3 through 12 of the periodic table, these are considered

47

Ag

Silver

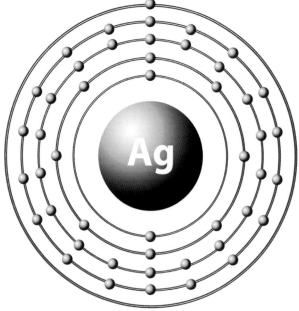

A diagram of a silver atom shows the nucleus and a crowded set of 47 electrons.

transition metals, which get that name from the fact that their properties are less predictable based on their position than other elements.

Silver on an Atomic Scale

Silver's 47 electrons revolve around the nucleus in five energy levels, which scientists refer to as orbitals. There are two electrons on the very first orbital, closest to the nucleus, and eight electrons on the second. Both the third and the fourth orbitals have 18 electrons each. The outermost orbital has just one electron.

When an atom of one element bonds with an atom of another element, electrons on the outermost orbitals are generally used. Transition metals are different, though. Electrons on other orbitals of a transition metal are sometimes involved in the bonding process.

By the Numbers

Because pure silver is so soft, for certain purposes it is sometimes combined with other metals to harden it. It is common to add copper to pure silver, and you might even own a piece of jewelry composed of 92.5 percent silver and 7.5 percent copper. That alloy is known as sterling silver. Scientists measure hardness on the Mohs scale, which ranges from 1 to 10. Talc (like the kind in some bath powders) measures 1, while diamonds measure 10. Interestingly, silver is closer to talc than to diamonds; it measures 2.5 on the Mohs scale.

Silver is only half as dense as gold but four times as dense as aluminum. That's why a gold ring feels so much heavier than a silver ring of the same size—and why a ring made out of aluminum would not feel very weighty or special.

47

Ag

Silver

This happens because when electrons are added to a transition metal's outermost orbital, the first tend to behave like normal electrons, but the rest don't. Instead they act like shielding electrons. Those are the electrons in other orbitals, which "shield" the valence electrons from the forces exerted by the nucleus. When that happens, electrons from other orbitals sometimes "step in."

Chemical bonding basics

Although silver does not combine readily with many other elements, in Chapter 3, you will read about what happens when it does.

Silver's Physical Properties

In addition to discussing silver's chemical properties (such as how its electrons behave), chemists examine its physical properties.

At room temperature, silver is a solid. In fact, all the metals except for mercury are solids at room temperature. Silver melts and becomes a liquid at a temperature of 1,763°F (962°C). At that temperature, any food you tried to bake would be incinerated immediately. That high melting point makes silver a very useful element for industrial purposes, because it keeps its strength and shape under punishingly hot conditions. When silver or any other metal melts it is described as molten. (If you enjoy gory historical facts, you might like to know that Mongol ruler Genghis Khan once killed an enemy by pouring molten silver in his eyes and mouth.) The boiling point of silver is 4,014°F (2,212°C).

Silver is a **malleable** metal. A piece of silver can be flattened into a sheet just .0025 inches thick. It's also very ductile, which means it can be stretched into thin wires. If you had just a half ounce of silver, you could stretch it into a wire more than a mile long. In addition to its high boiling point, silver's malleability and ductility make it very useful for industrial applications.

Silver can be stretched into very thin, flexible—yet quite strong—wires or strands.

Ag 47

Silver

Silver reflects light better than any other metal. While that is also a useful trait—in fact, true for any metal—one of the element's most important physical properties is its ability to conduct heat and electricity efficiently. If one part of a silver object is heated up, the electrons can then carry the heat quickly to other parts. That's why if you put a silver spoon in a cup of hot tea, the handle will get hot even though it's not submerged in the hot liquid.

In the case of electricity, when voltage is applied, the electrons begin to move. This creates an electrical current. Although silver is the best electrical conductor of all the metals, more often copper is used for industrial purposes, because it is much cheaper.

The drinker of this tea would feel the heat in the spoon and the silver glass holder.

A few factors can reduce silver's conductivity. Silver with impurities does not conduct heat or electricity as well as pure silver because impurities reduce electron flow. For example, tarnished silver does not conduct electricity well. Tarnish is the discoloration that results when silver comes into contact with sulfur compounds.

 Text-Dependent Questions

1. How many shells does an atom of silver have?

2. What can reduce silver's conductivity?

3. What is the Mohs scale?

Research Project

Make a list of all the transition metals. Besides the behavior of the electrons on their shells, research what else makes them different from other elements.

Silver and You

Some elements, like oxygen, are found in large quantities in the human body. Silver is not one of those elements. Only a small quantity of silver can typically be measured in any person's system. That silver comes from inhaling particles that

WORDS TO UNDERSTAND

enzyme   a chemical substance that helps cause natural processes (like digestion) in humans, animals, and plants

excrete   to eliminate or discharge waste products from the blood, tissues, or organs

ingest   to swallow or consume

ion   an atom or group of atoms that has a positive or negative electric charge from losing or gaining one or more electrons

toxic   poisonous or deadly

are present in the air around us. Sometimes we **ingest** silver from contaminated food or drinking water. We normally take in around 80 micrograms of silver a day, with half coming from our diet. The human body is very efficient at getting rid of that small amount. We naturally **excrete** more than 99 percent of the silver we ingest.

A few metals are essential for human health. The essential metals are part of one or more of the **enzymes** that our bodies need to stay alive and healthy. They include iron, zinc, copper, manganese, chromium, molybdenum, and selenium—but not silver. People do not need silver to be healthy.

Unlike metals such as mercury or lead, however, silver is not **toxic** to human beings. There is no proof that silver causes cancer or neurological damage like those other metals. You may have heard on the news that people suffered health problems in communities such as Flint, Michigan, because of lead in their water. Lead is known to cause kidney cancer. You may have also heard the expression "mad as a hatter." That expression was coined in the 19th century, when mercury was used in the hat-making business. Prolonged exposure to large quantities of the element caused dementia. Day-to-day contact with silver coins, cutlery, and other such items has no bad effects on the human body. If you are a factory worker and are exposed to silver dust or fumes on a constant basis, you might have some minor problems. Inhaling the dust or fumes regularly might irritate the inside of your nose, mouth, and throat as well as your eyes. A small number of people are allergic to silver and will break out in a rash if they touch it.

For hundreds of years silver was used to prevent wounds from getting infected. That worked because positively charged **ions** of silver can damage the cell walls of bacteria or disrupt other microbial activity. It was common for hospitals to use bandages infused with silver on ulcers and other serious wounds.

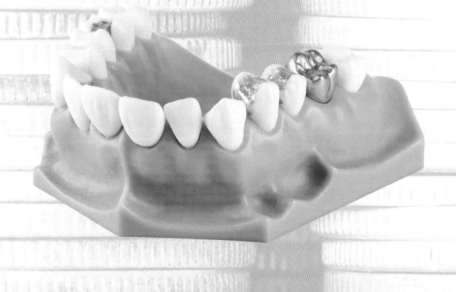

Burn victims were sometimes prescribed ointments containing silver. Newborn babies were given eye drops containing silver nitrate to prevent blindness.

In recent decades, though, doctors have been debating about how effective silver is, especially because better treatments are now widely available.

Many older people have dental fillings made of an alloy that contains mostly silver, with small amounts of copper, tin, zinc, and mercury. The older fillings often turned black, and dentists today use more advanced materials that work better.

One problem with putting silver compounds in medicines and supplements is that it sometimes causes the skin and mucous membranes to turn a sickly blue-gray color. That staining is called *argyria*. While argyria is merely cosmetic and doesn't pose any other health risks, it is permanent. The stain never goes away.

Federal agencies regulate how much silver people can safely be exposed to. The Environmental Protection Agency asks factory owners to report any spill or accident that releases more than 1,000 pounds of silver into the environment. The organization recommends that there be no more than 0.1 milligrams of silver in a liter of drinking water. There are also rules concerning workplace air, which should not have more than .01 milligrams per cubic meter.

47
Ag
Silver

WORDS TO UNDERSTAND

allotrope   different physical forms in which an element can exist

gelatin   a colorless and tasteless, water-soluble protein prepared from collagen

precipitate   a solid substance that separates from a solution

Silver Combines

Compounds are formed when atoms of different elements join together. This happens through chemical reactions. You read about orbital electrons in the chapter on silver's physical and chemical properties. Chemical bonds are formed when atoms transfer or share orbital electrons. Silver is relatively unreactive, however. That means it does not bond well or easily with other elements or compounds.

Silver and Oxygen

While most other metals react naturally with the oxygen (O_2) in the air, silver does not. It does react with a common **allotrope** of oxygen called ozone (O_3), and when that

47
Ag
Silver

happens, it forms a compound called silver oxide (Ag$_2$O), a dark-colored powder that can be used for many industrial purposes, including making batteries.

Iron reacts to the oxygen in the air and forms rust. While silver doesn't rust, it will get discolored when it reacts to other substances. You read earlier that if silver is exposed to sulfur (element number 16 on the periodic table), it will become blackened or tarnished. This is because sulfur-containing substances in the air combine with the silver to form silver sulfide (Ag$_2$S). Silver sulfide is black. You can get rid of the tarnish on a piece of silver jewelry or household item by rubbing off the layer of silver sulfide with a cloth. You can also actually reverse the chemical reaction that caused the silver sulfide to form.

Silver can become tarnished with silver sulfide when exposed to air.

Noble Metals

After forming compounds, silver can return to its uncombined state relatively easily. Because of this trait, it is called a "noble metal." Other noble metals are ruthenium, rhodium, palladium, osmium, iridium, platinum, and gold. These are metals that strongly resist oxidation. (They are the opposite of the base metals, like iron, which readily react to the oxygen in the air.) Because there are no definite rules about how resistant a metal has to be to qualify as noble, scientists disagree about exactly what metals should be on the list. Some think mercury, rhenium, and copper should be included, too.

Aluminum reacts more easily with sulfur than silver does. If you place the tarnished piece of silver, such as a fork or candlestick, in a solution of baking soda along with a piece of aluminum foil, you can watch this happen. Aluminum sulfide will form, and you will see small yellow flakes in the bottom of your pan. The silver and aluminum have to be touching for this to work, because a small electric current flows between them during the reaction.

47
Ag
Silver

The Halides

Silver reacts readily to the nonmetallic elements from group 17 on the periodic table. These are called halogens, which means "salt-formers." Any compound that contains a halogen is called a salt. The halogens are fluorine, chlorine, bromine, iodine, astatine, and ununseptium. All halogens have seven electrons in their outer orbitals.

Silver plays a part in the making of many types of photographic film.

When silver reacts with one of the halogens, it forms a silver halide. These include silver bromide (AgBr), silver chloride (AgCl), silver iodide (AgI), and three different forms of silver fluoride. Sometimes the whole group is referred to as AgX, although that is not really an actual chemical symbol. It is easy to identify silver bromide, chloride, and iodide in the lab. The first produces a cream-colored **precipitate** in solution. Silver chloride's precipitate is white. Silver iodide produces a yellowish precipitate.

Because the silver halides are very sensitive to light, they have many uses. One of the most important uses is the manufacture of X-ray film as well as film used to take photos. To make film, the silver halide is formed into tiny microcrystals and suspended in **gelatin**. A thin layer of the gelatin mixture is applied to a glass plate or flexible piece of plastic or paper.

The X-ray film is now covered with silver ions. When the film is exposed to light, the electrons in it are energized and the silver ions are transformed back into atoms. Silver atoms are black, so an exposed piece of film turns black at each point where light has hit a silver ion. In a way, a photo is simply a picture that has been drawn with silver

instead of pen or pencil. About 5,000 photos can be taken using just one ounce of silver.

Silver halide-based photography is becoming much more rare because of the popularity of digital photography.

A thin silver coating on the inside of these glass balls creates a shine.

Silver halides are made with the help of another silver compound, silver nitrate ($AgNo_3$), which forms when silver reacts with nitric acid (HNO_3). This reaction happens because nitric acid contains negatively charged nitrate ions and positively charged hydrogen ions. When silver is added, the silver atoms each give up one electron to form ions with a positive charge. One positively charged silver ion combines with a negatively charged nitrate ion, and a molecule of silver nitrate is formed.

It's Complicated

Some silver compounds are very complex and contain many elements, as you can see from their chemical symbols. For example, the chemical symbol for silver fulminate is

Silver can be a part of the small explosions created by these popular party poppers.

$Ag_2C_2N_2O_2$, which tells us that it contains silver, carbon, nitrogen, and oxygen. Silver fulminate is highly explosive. If you had a small pile of the compound, even the weight of a single drop of water would be enough to detonate it. (You would never have a large pile, because the compound self-detonates under its own weight.) If you've ever played with a "party popper" or other small firecracker, it probably contained a very minute amount of silver fulminate.

Another useful silver compound is silver sulfadiazine, which contains carbon, hydrogen, silver, nitrogen, oxygen, and sulfur. This is one of the compounds used in burn ointments and other medications.

47

Ag

Silver

Hand lotion and hand sanitizing gels are just some of the products that include ethylene oxide, which silver plays a part in manufacturing.

In addition to participating in its own reactions, silver sometimes acts as a catalyst, helping reactions between other elements to take place without being affected itself. A catalyst is like a jump-starter; it makes things happen chemically while remaining unchanged. Consider the compound ethylene oxide, which is very important in the plastics industry. It could not be made without silver. When silver is added to ethylene (C_2H_2) and oxygen (O_2), the oxygen molecule breaks apart. The two oxygen atoms bind weakly to the surface of the silver.

When an ethylene molecule comes into contact with the silver, the oxygen atoms respond. One oxygen atom joins one ethylene molecule to form ethylene oxide. Formaldehyde (CH_2O) is another important industrial chemical that is formed with the help of silver as a catalyst.

 Text-Dependent Questions

1. To which allotrope of oxygen does silver readily react?

2. What color is silver sulfide?

3. Name an industrial chemical that is formed with the help of silver as a catalyst.

Research Project

Silver halides are very important in photography. Make a timeline detailing the major events and advances in the history of photography.

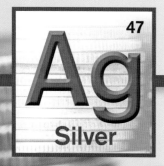

Ag 47

Silver

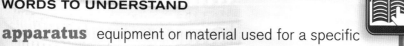

WORDS TO UNDERSTAND

apparatus equipment or material used for a specific purpose or job

colloidal describes a substance that consists of particles suspended within another substance

obsidian a hard, dark, glass-like volcanic rock

photovoltaic the production of electric current at the intersection of two substances that have been exposed to light

Silver in
Our World

n addition to being a noble metal, silver is considered a precious metal. Many people think precious metals and noble metals are the same. Even though some metals qualify as both, they are two different things. Precious metals are rare, naturally occurring elements with a high financial value. They are usually less reactive than other elements, have an attractive luster, and are ductile. (Remember that ductile substances have the ability to be stretched into thin wires.) Besides silver, the list of precious metals includes gold and all the elements in the platinum group: iridium, osmium, palladium, platinum, rhodium, and ruthenium.

Minerals that are made of atoms of a single element are referred to as native elements, but silver is rarely found by itself, as a native element mineral. Most silver produced today is in-

stead a by-product of mining base metals like copper and zinc. When that happens, the value of the small amounts of silver can be greater than the value of the primary metal within the ore.

Formed in Supernovae

Scientists who study the origins of everything in the universe explain that light elements, like helium, were formed during an event called the Big Bang, a massive cosmic explosion. Heavy elements, like carbon, were formed within stars, through nuclear fusion. Nuclear fusion is a process in which multiple nuclei join together to form a heavier nucleus. They believe that rare metals like gold and silver were formed during the explosions of massive stars called supernovae.

To learn how silver was created, they used computer modeling and discovered that the hotter and denser the star, the more metal is produced. Silver-producing supernovae were plentiful, but each star might have ejected very little metal (in some cases, a billionth of the original mass of the star).

From that explosive cosmic origin, silver has come to play a big part in everyday life.

Double silver: This mirror has a handle made of silver as well as silver in its surface.

Mirrors

Just think of how many times a day you look into or walk by a mirror. In ancient times, people used polished **obsidian** to make mirrors. Later, they began to polish thin sheets of gold, silver, and aluminum instead.

In Venice, in about 1600, the "silvering process" was invented, and it is still used in modern times. Venetian glassmakers discovered that if they coated the back of a sturdy piece of glass with mercury, the reflection produced was nearly perfect. They chose glass, as we still do today, because it was transparent and rigid. It was also easy to smooth out and cut. (Smoothness is very important, because any imperfections in the glass will cause the reflection to be wavy or distorted.) Today, however, instead of mercury, silver or aluminum is generally used. (Remember, mercury is very toxic.)

47

Ag

Silver

There are many ways to coat glass with silver or some other metal to make a mirror. In one factory method, smooth pieces of glass are placed on an electric conveyor belt. A special **apparatus** cleans off oils or dirt. The glass is rinsed with deionized water. Deionized water has any ions from soil or plumbing pipes removed so that they don't cause unwanted chemical reactions. Next, liquefied tin is applied to one side of the glass to help the silver stick. After the liquefied silver

Silver is formed into jewelry of just about any imaginable shape and style.

is spread on top of the tin, the extra is wiped away and can be reused. Finally, a layer of paint is applied as a final coat to protect the silver. The mirror is then heated at high temperatures to evaporate any moisture and is ready to be used.

Jewelry and Other Decorative Items

Archaeologists have discovered large troves of decorative silver objects made by the ancient Romans, and there have even been cases of ordinary farmers coming across Roman silver while plowing their fields. In 1830, for example, a French farmer discovered "the Berthouville Treasure," which consisted of statuettes and vessels. Later, in 1942, the "Mildenhall Treasure" was found by a British farmer. It it contained ornate platters, bowls, and ladles whose handles were made to look like dolphins. In some ways, we aren't so different from the ancient Romans. We are still using silver to adorn ourselves and our homes, thanks to its beauty and durability.

Silver is graded according to its purity, and if you look at a piece of sterling silver jewelry, you might see a mark reading 925. That means it has a purity of 92.5 percent. Sometimes less expensive pieces are

47

Ag

Silver

made with 80 percent pure silver, but those pieces would not be called sterling. (The word sterling probably comes from the old English *steorling*, which referred to a small coin used in England during the Medieval Period.)

Because silver is expensive, sometimes manufacturers use silver plating instead. The process of silver plating was discovered in 1742 by a British craftsman named Thomas Bolsover. By accident, he overheated a knife made of silver and copper. The silver formed a shiny layer over the copper. He realized that it would be cheaper to produce cutlery with just a thin layer of silver on top of a less costly metal. He called his technique Sheffield plating after the name of his town.

In 1840, brothers named George and Henry Elkington discovered a new and better technique. They immersed items made of copper, nickel, or zinc in a solution containing silver ions. The submersed item became part of an electrical circuit. As electrons flowed through the circuit, the silver ions moved towards the item (which acted as a negative electrode) and picked up an electron. Silver atoms were formed and adhered to the item. The process became known as electroplating and is still used today.

Coinage

Archaeologists believe that the ancient Egyptians were the first people to use pieces of silver to trade for goods, starting around 3000 BCE. By 500 BCE coins were being minted (stamped out

Rare examples of American silver dollars like this one can fetch millions at coin auctions.

of metal) and used as official coinage. From the end of the Roman Empire through the 16th century, silver was the main metal used in coinage.

The United States minted its first silver coin in 1772. To mint a coin, a government first asks an artist to create the design that will appear on it. That design is then used to make a tool called a "die." Blank, round discs are cut out of a sheet of polished metal. The die is then used to stamp the design onto the disc. Finally, the finished coins are inspected, counted, and sent out for distribution.

Ag 47

Silver

As silver got more and more expensive, the amount in the coins was gradually decreased in favor of cheaper metals. Finally, in 1965, the U.S. stopped using silver entirely. (Dimes, for example, are now made from an alloy of copper and nickel.) Other countries have done the same. Today, only Mexico continues to place silver coins in general circulation.

However, countries still mint beautiful silver coins meant as collectors' items. The U.S. Mint makes the "Silver Eagle," a one-ounce coin with a face value of a dollar. Created from 99.9 percent pure silver, it features an eagle on one side and a woman in a flowing gown on the other. Canada offers a similarly collectible coin called the "Silver Maple Leaf," and Australia has the "Silver Kookaburra."

The famous Morgan silver dollars got their name from the engraver, George Morgan.

Older coins are also popular with collectors. For example, the Morgan silver dollar, a silver coin minted in the

U.S. between 1878 and 1921, is highly sought after.

When people buy silver as an investment they refer to its weight in troy ounces. The name comes from the medieval town of Troyes, France, where the system of measurement

US Mint tour

originated. One troy ounce weighs 31.1034 grams. That is about 10 percent more than a regular ounce.

Batteries in Space

Many batteries now include silver alloys. Although these can be more expensive than common lithium batteries, they are considered very reliable, efficient, and better for the environment. The small, button-like batteries used in watches, calculators, and hearing aids contain silver oxide. They are about one-third silver by weight.

Silver batteries are very good at storing a lot of energy in a very small area. Because of this they have even been used on spacecraft. That's not the only purpose silver has served on space missions,

though. More than 20,000 silver-coated quartz tiles were used to protect NASA's *Magellan* spacecraft (launched in 1989) from solar radiation. The panels kept the craft's sophisticated electronics from becoming overheated when it orbited Venus. Silver was chosen because it reflects light so well and is also resistant to corrosion.

Electronics

Almost all of the electronic devices we use every day include silver in some capacity, because it conducts electricity better than any other element. Electronics manufacturers often make their products with silver membrane switches. Unlike a mechanical switch, a membrane switch consists of a circuit printed on a piece of optoelectronic material.

Consider your computer keyboard. Under each key are two tiny patches of silver, with a small space between them. Pressing a key makes the two pieces touch, and an electrical current flows to the computer's central processing unit (CPU). Because the silver is sensitive, you only have to touch the keyboard lightly in order for the letters to appear on your screen. Silver's durability means that you can acti-

Circuit boards used in a vast array of electronics include silver among their elemental components.

vate the switch millions and millions of times without it breaking or wearing out. Silver membrane switches are used in televisions, microwaves, cell phones, toys, and a multitude of other products.

Circuit boards also use silver. A circuit board is a piece of insulating material (almost always green in color) threaded with conductive wires and other components. When a power supply sends an electrical charge to the board, it flows along the wires and controls the functions of the device. The components are attached to the board with a silver alloy, called solder (pronounced SAH-der), which allows the electricity to flow freely. Boards are now sometimes even printed with conductive silver-based ink that can replace bulky wires.

Making the World Cleaner and Greener

Using silver for water purification is not a new idea. Phoenicians, a seafaring people who lived around the time of the ancient Greeks,

47

Ag

Silver

preserved their water and wine during long ocean voyages by storing it in silver vessels. Hundreds of years later, American settlers placed silver coins in their water barrels to keep the water pure.

Today, silver is an important component in many home water purifiers. Tiny silver particles are embedded into the material used in the filter. These prevent bacteria and algae from building up, so that the

Silver is a key ingredient in solar cells that turn sunlight into electricity and energy.

unit can work efficiently to strain out lead, chlorine, and other things people don't want in their drinking water. Silver is now also being used in some public water towers and in hospital water systems to control the *Legionella* bacteria, which has caused multiple outbreaks of deadly disease. Some tech-savvy swimming pool owners are even installing electrical ionizing units that use silver as an alternative to chlorine. The U.S. Centers for Disease Control and Prevention says that low-tech ceramic filters infused with **colloidal** silver are of great help in the developing world. Regions that use the filters have reduced gastrointestinal diseases considerably.

We now know that solar energy is an environmentally friendly and cost-effective way to generate power. Drive through certain areas, and you will see many buildings—from large businesses to single-family homes—with solar panels on their roofs. Those panels contain **photovoltaic** cells that capture the sun's rays and transform them into energy. Silver is an important ingredient in making those cells. Almost all of them, no matter where they were made, contain silver paste. Industry experts estimate that 70 million ounces of silver are used each year by the manufacturers of solar panels.

Other Technology

All the uses for silver that have been discovered in recent decades could fill several books. Some sources even claim that there are more than 10,000 uses of silver in industrial applications.

Just a few of the most interesting, innovative, and imaginative are:

- Radio frequency identification tags, which are attached to products to prevent theft or track inventory, use silver-based inks.
- Silver-based inks are also used in prepaid toll passes.
- Many CDs and DVDs are coated with silver.
- Silver iodide (one of the halides) can be dropped into clouds from airplanes. The process, called cloud seeding, causes rain to fall in dry areas, so crops can grow.
- Museum curators can test whether a material will damage delicate artworks by placing a sample of it in an airtight jar that also contains silver. This is called the "Oddy Test," after its inventor, Andrew Oddy.
- Silver film is used to make the automatic defrosters on some car windshields.
- A washing machine has entered the market that coats clothes

Silver combines with aluminum to make the skin of this Apache helicopter.

with a layer of silver ions, reportedly leaving them odor-free and bacteria-resistant.

- High-tech athletic clothing is being made from fabrics already containing silver nanoparticles that fight sweat and smells.
- Some personal-care companies are adding silver chloride to their deodorants, claiming that it makes them more effective.
- A silver coating is applied on the surface of infrared telescope mirrors for greater reflectivity and reduced heat emission.
- A strong silver-aluminum alloy is used in the Army's Apache helicopter, as well as in other military vehicles.
- The rods in nuclear reactors that control the fission rate of radioactive materials like uranium and plutonium are made partially of silver.

Ag 47

Silver

The Silver Institute is a global business association. The organization estimates that in one year alone, more than 225 million ounces of silver are used by jewelry makers. Pure silver coins and bars purchased by collectors and investors take almost 300 million ounces. Even though electronic devices use minuscule amounts of silver, when you add them together, they total some 250 million ounces per year. More minor uses include cutlery, photographic film, and photovoltaic panels.

Mexico now tops the list of silver-producing countries, with about 190 million ounces mined and refined annually. The U.S. is further down on that

Silver from Mexico is often turned into beautiful jewelry that reflects native traditions.

list, producing approximately 35 million ounces. Global production now averages about 670 million ounces per year.

Since ancient cultures first began mining silver some 5,000 years ago, the element has been used for the benefit of humankind. It's easy to imagine that 5,000 years from now, people will still be using it.

 ## Text-Dependent Questions

1. What is the Mildenhall Treasure and when was it discovered?

2. What spacecraft included silver-covered tiles?

3. How many ounces of silver are used each year by the manufacturers of solar panels?

Research Project

Do you think deodorants made with silver are really more effective? How about high-tech athletic clothing with silver nanoparticles? Try to find consumer reviews for at least three products that contain silver. Write a paragraph explaining why you might or might not purchase the products.

FIND OUT MORE

Books

Aldersey-Williams, Hugh. *Periodic Tales: A Cultural History of the Elements, From Arsenic to Zinc.* New York: Ecco Press, 2011. This book contains true stories of the fascinating, but mysterious, building blocks of the universe—the elements.

Browne, John. *Seven Elements That Have Changed the World.* New York: Pegasus Books, 2015. This book details how iron, carbon, gold, silver, uranium, titanium, and silicon each had a part in shaping human civilization, both for good and for ill.

Kean, Sam. *The Disappearing Spoon: And Other True Tales of Madness, Love, and the History of the World From the Periodic Table of the Elements.* Boston: Back Bay Books, 2010. This book has been praised for its incredible stories of science, history, finance, mythology, the arts, medicine, and more, all involving the elements.

Websites

www.silverinstitute.org
The website of the Silver Institute offers information on silver metal in industrial use, global silver exchange rates, technology, photography, medicine and jewelry.

periodic.lanl.gov/47.shtml
This page from the Los Alamos National Laboratory contains useful basic information about silver and the other elements.

www.chemicool.com/elements/silver.html
The Chemicool website offers fun facts, science history, and more.

SERIES GLOSSARY OF KEY TERMS

carbohydrates a group of organic compounds including sugars, starches, and fiber

conductivity the ability of a substance for heat or electricity to pass through it

inert unable to bond with other matter

ion an atom with an electrical charge due to the loss or gain of an electron

isotope an atom of a specific element that has a different number of neutrons; it has the same atomic number but a different mass

nuclear fission process by which a nucleus is split into smaller parts releasing massive amounts of energy

nuclear fusion process by which two atomic nuclei combine to form a heavier element while releasing energy

organic compound a chemical compound in which one or more atoms of carbon are linked to atoms of other elements (most commonly hydrogen, oxygen, or nitrogen)

solubility the ability of a substance to dissolve in a liquid

spectrum the range of electromagnetic radiation with respect to its wavelength or frequency; can sometimes be observed by characteristic colors or light

INDEX

Photo Credits

Adobe Images: auremar 7, blueringmedia 8, 24, destina 10, waj 14, Bukhta79 16, Nevio3 18, RTImages 25, Mikhail Ulyannikov 27, Oksana Churakova 28, Zea Lenanet 31, photocall 36, Focalpoint 41, justinkendra 44, pixelrobot 47, gavran333 51, Radnatt 52, luckylight 55, smileus 56. Dreamstime.com: Lane Erickson 12, Luis Alvarenga, Macker54321 34, Remik44992 38, Ksya 40, David Schliepp 42. 1stdibs.com: 19. Flickr: Ken Lund 20. National Museum of American History, National Numismatic Collection: 51. Shutterstock: Smereka 22. US Navy: 59.

About the Author

Mari Rich was educated at Lehman College, part of the public City University of New York. As a writer and editor, she has had many years of experience in the fields of university communications and reference publishing, most notably with the highly regarded periodical *Current Biography*, aimed at high school and college readers. She also edited and wrote for *World Authors, Leaders of the Information Age,* and *Nobel Laureates*. Currently, she spends much of her time writing about engineers and engineering.